DINOSAUR ISLAND

BY MAX HAYNES

LOTHROP, LEE & SHEPARD BOOKS ◆ NEW YORK

Legend says that once a year,
on the day between summer and fall,
an island of dinosaurs will appear.
Maddy and Bing set off to find it.

They sailed at dawn from Maddy's cabin on Messenger Lake,
up through Drew Channel, and into Rex Bay.
There they found a place they had never seen before.
Bing marked the spot on their map,
and Maddy named it Dinosaur Island.

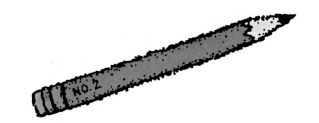

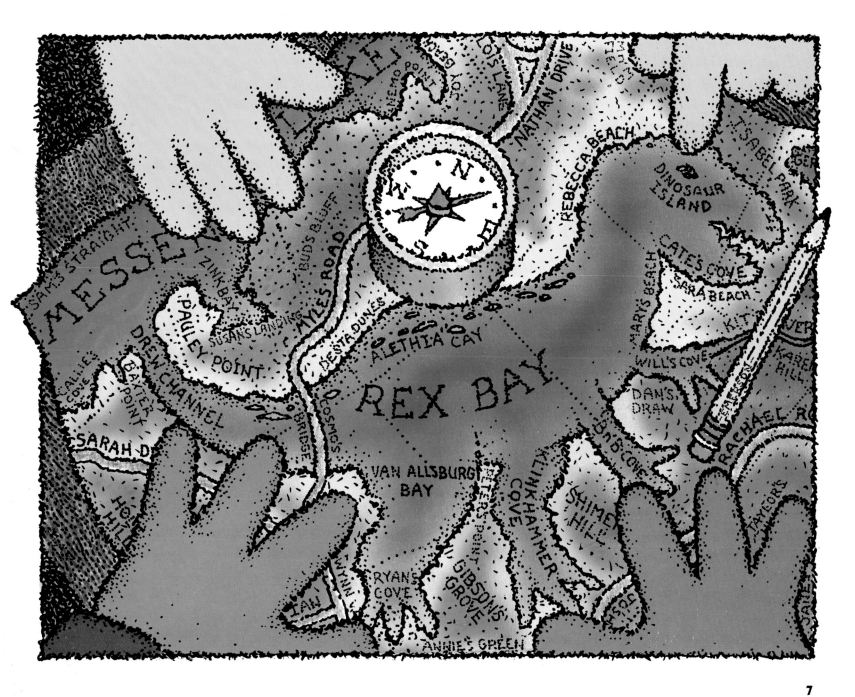

"Something tells me
this must be the place," said Bing.
"This will be fun!" said Maddy.

They found a good spot to drop anchor,
then waded ashore.
Maddy set off right away,
looking for dinosaur tracks,
but Bing took his time.
He thought he saw something move
in a pile of rocks,
but it was only rabbits.

11

Then he thought he saw something move
in the air above him,
but it was just birds.

Then he thought he saw something move
over in the hills,
but it was just some bears.

"BEARS!" screamed Maddy.
"RUN FOR THE WOODS, BING!"

Luckily, when the bear and her cubs
reached the edge of the forest,
they stopped short.
"I wonder why they did that," said Maddy.
"Who knows," whispered Bing.
"Maybe they saw a dinosaur."

19

"You mean like these dinosaur squirrels?"
teased Maddy.
"Of course not," said Bing
as he stopped to rest on an old log.
"Dinosaurs are big enough to sit on."

They continued their search, but without any luck.
"Maybe we should climb these rocks," said Maddy.
"This way looks safer," said Bing.
"Okay," replied Maddy,
"but I think we might see a lot from up there."

So they followed a stream
until it came to an unusual waterfall.
"Do you get the feeling
that we're being watched?" whispered Bing.
"Only by bees and butterflies," said Maddy.

Bing sighed.

"You're probably right," he said.

"I guess it's time to head back to the boat.

Before it gets dark."

So they set sail for home.

"That sure was fun," said Maddy.

"Yeah," said Bing,

"but it's too bad we didn't see any dinosaurs."

Did you see a dinosaur?

P.S. Maybe you saw a dinosaur and maybe you didn't!
Plesiosaurs, Pterodactyls, and Dimetrodons are ancient reptiles;
they are not true dinosaurs.

TO MY LOVELY WIFE, JANE

First Edition 1 2 3 4 5 6 7 8 9 10

Library of Congress Cataloging in Publication Data
Haynes, Max. Dinosaur Island / Max Haynes.
p.   cm.   Summary: Maddy and Bing take off in their little boat to find Dinosaur Island, which only appears once a year. ISBN 0-688-10329-4 (trade). — ISBN 0-688-10330-8 (library)
[1. Explorers—Fiction. 2. Dinosaurs—Fiction.] I. Title. PZ7.H314914Di 1991 [E]—dc20
90-48148 CIP AC